Facebook.com/BeTheParentYouWishYouHad

"Every parent should read this."

    -   my aunt, an educator for 45 years

"It's great. Draw some cartoons for it."

    -   my mom

"Can I share this with my girlfriend?"

    -   a divorcing father, after he finished reading a draft of my book. He initially approached me after attending my workshop. I shared the book with him since he was going through a hard time.

"We've read your book three times."

    -   good friends who are raising their beautiful son in Abuja, Nigeria.

Be the Parent
You Wish You Had

For All Parents & Grandparents

Written & Illustrated
by Mother Zeus

New Orange Press
New York

Dedicated to my Dad

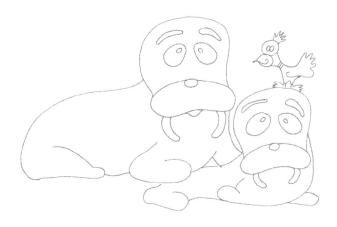

New Orange Press
New York
Copyright © 2016 by Mother Zeus

MotherZeus1@gmail.com
facebook.com/BeTheParentYouWishYouHad

About the Author

Mother Zeus's motivation for writing this book is to help kids have better lives with their families. Mother Zeus loves children way more than grown-ups.

Mother Zeus considered becoming a children's rights lawyer but did not have the stomach for fighting. So instead, she became a teacher for 25 years, a school administrator for 4 and is currently both the director of a university's teacher education program and a teacher in an enrichment program for forward-thinking teenagers in Harlem who will attend superb colleges.

She has taught every grade but first and twelfth, with nine years of teaching children under five. In the past few years, she has been busy painting school murals in the Bronx and Harlem, teaching kids of all ages and mentoring teachers.

Mother Zeus is a mother and a godmother.

Contents

Introduction

The big & little creatures we call our kids can be our greatest sources for fun or our most fierce foes. They are in our care for nearly two decades, and no two days are the same.

When we were kids, we fantasized about our dream parents. Now maybe we can become the parent we always wanted to have.

What experience are your kids having with you as their parent?
Put yourself in your kids' shoes. Imagine walking in their footsteps. See yourself through their eyes. If all the parents you know were lined up, would you have chosen yourself as a parent?

I've been an educator for three decades. Along the way, I've met thousands of families. And much to my distress, too many parents view their children as problems to be solved rather than as sources of joy and pleasure. How can we change this up? How can we make those two decades of nearly full-time parenthood super fun?

All parents need is a positive mindset and a bag of tricks in their repertoire. After thirty years in education as a teacher, dean, admissions director, mentor, school muralist, and parent advisor as well as twenty years as a parent, I would like to share some good stuff that works.

Our Kids Want a Parent, Not a Friend

What do you look for in a leader? Someone who is honest, knowledgeable, calm and filled with ideas.

You are your child's leader.

During my first teaching job, I had a sixth grade student named Asher. Every day, he attempted a full-scale mutiny with his refusal to, in his words, "take orders." In his mind, he was in charge, he talked back, he did not accept that anyone had more knowledge than him.

When I spoke to his parents, they said, "We view Asher as a roommate rather than our child. He calls us by our first names instead of mom and dad."

Asher, a twelve year-old, was not equipped to be an equal among adults, so he lashed out at his teachers and parents to assert his strength.

Think back to your childhood. Did you want to be friends with the adults around you?

Kids don't want their parents to be their friends. They already have plenty of friends. Kids want authority figures they can trust. And kids want the grown folks to be on their side, on their team.

So much of parenting involves conjuring up the memories of when we were kids. How did we view adults? How did it feel when an adult spoke to us?

Ideally, parents are family leaders, the sources of love, care and the transfer of wisdom.

Strict & Fair & Really Kind

When I asked a class of sixth graders to
create their own social contract, they wanted
to include their expectations for me, their
teacher. They wrote that they wanted me to
be "strict and fair and really kind." The
students knew from experience that a
teacher who is too kind may not be able to
provide the structure of a strict teacher. My
students craved the freedom in the
classroom that comes when there is the
order and clear expectations of a strict
teacher. But they were clear; they did not
want a stern, humorless teacher.

I have taught every grade but first grade and
twelfth grade. For seven years, I taught
children under age five. Of all of the
thousands of children I have taught, no
matter the age, kids crave justice. My sixth
graders wrote it down in the rules. They
wanted me to be fair in the classroom.

But more than anything else, the students
expressed that they sought a "really kind"
teacher to implement order and justice.
True kindness derives from empathy.

Visualize what it was like when you were a kid. Frequently remind yourself of those feelings. You too would likely want an adult who speaks clearly, defines expectations, lacks rigidity and has a warm, kind heart.

Strict parents create predictable rules that their children knows in advance. In a calm moment when all is going well, tell your children how you will deal with their negative behavior. With my own kids, I told them many times, "If you're good, you get good. If you're bad, you get bad." The simplicity of the sentence worked from the terrible twos until their teens.

One afternoon, I bought my four year-old a calendar with photographs of antique cars. He pored over every page at the bookstore gushing over the colors and design. He told me just where he would hang it in his bedroom. On the way home, we stopped at the grocery store. He pointed out some junk food that he wanted to buy, and I said no. In the grocery store line, he stamped his feet, cried and then lay on the floor. This tactic did not produce what he wanted. So he encircled his arms around my legs to entrap me. I could only take tiny steps. I ignored him, and his arms tightened. I took mini steps until I reached the cashier. After I paid, I shuffled along and said calmly to my son as he was still holding tightly to my legs, "See this beautiful calendar? You see how you are behaving? Say goodbye to the calendar." I threw it in the trash, and he released my legs as the tears poured. After a few minutes, he calmed down, and we went home.

How did I keep my cool during this public tantrum? Whenever times were rough, I pretended that I was the best-paid babysitter. I would think to myself, "I get $1,000 an hour. I have to keep calm to keep this job." My imaginary job requirement was maintaining a kind of detached serenity rather than sliding into that impulsive bull-charging red flag of parental fury.

After my son's tears stopped, that was his last tantrum for a long stretch. My son asserted his strength with anger, and I asserted mine with calm. The consequence for his behavior inflicted just enough pain that my son understood that, in the field of battle, he would lose something valuable.

Crimes & Consequences

We are only partially free. We need to behave well in social situations and learn to follow reasonable directives.

We do not want our children to follow every directive they are given. Otherwise, our children will grow up to be sheep who do not think for themselves.

At the same time, the creation of a positive climate with expectations for good behavior is crucial. Children are more likable both to themselves and others when they are cooperative and respectful. As parents try to shape their kids into civilized beings, the kids may resist.

Parent: *Do what I say. Now.*
Child: *No.*

Children, the aspiring adults-in-training, want to be in charge just as badly as their parents. And when that little squirt demands to be in charge, parents flame into an apoplectic rage.

When parents are confronted, they need to avoid personalizing this very normal rejection and rebellion. Like a good leader, parents need to set a calm tone and maintain their understanding that the aim of a punishment is to deter the child from repeating what was done. The child's negative behaviors need swift, clear consequences.

The punishment for children should ideally be something that benefits the parent. If your child neglects to text from her friend's house when she arrives there, she will need to vacuum the house when she gets home. Once the vacuuming is finished, the child has done her time and the parent should not extend the consequence by harping on the punished deed. Move on and hope for progress the next time. Ideally, the consequence for negative behaviors is already established and known before the misdeed. However, parents reserve the right to have consequences for unforeseen infractions. And remember, if you make the threat, you gotta' follow through.
Sometimes children are itching for a fight. One of my students named Fred refused to

line up. He would dance around, shout, lie on the floor and sing. He craved a face-to-face battle. Looking at him, saying his name or engaging in an argument would be like giving him a reward. Instead, I praised the rest of the class for lining up. I told them that we were going on a great adventure. We would pretend to be cats hunting mice. We better find some because our food supply was low. The defiant little Fred found his way into the line. Then I said, "Fred, maybe you can be on the look-out for cheese!" Once he was cooperating, I was quick to positively involve him in the imaginative play.

Children can be convinced to cooperate when parents create a fun, appealing scenario. Being persuasive can also make the child want to cooperate. Think Tom Sawyer and the painting of his fence. Consequences will make your child think twice before repeating the negative behavior. Without consequences, many of us would not wait at red lights or pay our taxes. But consequences for our kids should not be severe. Instead, they should be effective and edifying.

Positive Attracts Positive

Remember when you were a kid and you could tell which adults liked you and which adults didn't? You knew who was the favored one in your family or who were the teachers' pets. The adults revealed their true feelings through their tone, eyes and facial expressions. It was obvious.

Maybe as an adult you think that kids cannot figure out how you feel, who you favor and when you are dissatisfied. But as a species we are wired to know what people are thinking. It has helped us survive, and we rely on our ability to read other people's emotions.

Kids pick up on everything. They need to gather loads of information on the road to competent adulthood. They are wired to be as observant as a savvy scientist and as absorbent as a sea sponge.

Kids know which teachers chose the profession so they could have summers off. They know which teachers got into the field because they love the sparkling, kinetic minds of young people.

The children's experiences with the two types of teachers are so vastly different. The ones who just punch the clock are counting the days until the first day of summer vacation. The others treat the children with warmth, love, and respect.

Parents also convey a range of emotions to their children. Different children spark different feelings. I come from a family of four children.

The genetic cocktails that created the four of us were shaken and stirred to create a wide range of personalities. Introverted, outgoing, artistic, scientific, funny, serious. We knew which one our parents favored and who triggered their short fuse.

As parents, we choose to have children for a variety of reasons. If we were running on pure gratitude, once our children are born, their very existence would be enough to satisfy us. In the animal world this seems to be the case. But in the human world, children can be made to feel that they are on earth to satisfy their parents' exceedingly high expectations. Very often, what a child lacks is emphasized much more than what the child contributes.

When parents adopt a positive mind frame by accepting and appreciating their children as they are, the children gain the confidence of feeling that they have "made it." They do not need to accomplish something to be accepted. The children are living with the home team, their parents, who are rooting for them and on their side.

Yes, children need to practice piano, take out the trash, and study for their math quizzes. They do have responsibilities, just as adults do. But these are activities and not who they are. A positive outlook sees what is there rather than what is not. This fosters an atmosphere of acceptance and adoration. Children should never feel they need to do something to earn your love and approval. They already have it when they get out of bed in the morning and when they go to sleep at night.

Anger is a Whip. Keep Cool.

When your child infuriates you, try to suppress this fury.

The signs of anger are typically a raised, hostile voice that aims to induce fear, like when dogs snarl to keep you off their territory. In a way, bringing out anger is like whipping out an invisible but pain-inducing weapon to defeat the opponent.

But so often, we feel that anger bursting forth.

Use different strategies to lower your anger temperature. Think thoughts like, "$1,000 an hour babysitters don't act hostile. Calm down or you may lose this great gig. Breathe. Your employer may have a nanny camera aimed right at you. Cool it or face the unemployment line."

I'm telling you, these babysitter thoughts made me so relaxed that parents would often ask me, "How are you so chilled out?" It's because when times got tough, I played the role of the most nurturing, no-nonsense nanny in town.

Embrace your role as a role model of communication that is clear and calm. After all, we do not want our kids to think anger is acceptable in a family. Otherwise, they will then use anger in interactions with their future partners and children. Express yourself with a voice that is determined but not loud and hostile.

When I worked in high need public schools, I was surrounded by screaming teachers. They lost control of themselves and used righteous fury to try to restrain their gigantic, rebellious class of students.

But I chose to never raise my voice with my ninety-nine students split into three classes. I used a hushed and serious tone to provide simple guidelines for the students. Sit up straight, feet flat on the floor, pencils ready, let's learn. Sometimes, students shouted, threatened and cursed at me. At those moments, I pictured an alternative version of the child, one that was living in a welcoming, dignified and positive environment. Ignoring the student's negative tone, I responded with good manners and calm.

When confronted, I would often agree with my students and let them know that I understood their point. They felt listened to and well-regarded. Eventually, their calmer selves expressed their thoughts in a more relaxed, friendly tone. Sometimes, this took loads of time. But when progress was made, they were praised at every step forward.

One student asked me, "Why don't you yell? Why don't you get in our faces?"

I responded that I want a healthy, joyful life and screaming is not a part of that. I also said that I want to be proud of the person I see in the mirror every morning. If I screamed, I would not like myself.

When we feel anger boiling forth, we can use time as our ally. In a rough moment, we can calmly say, "I will need time to think about how to deal with this." Be confident enough to resist being impulsive. Take time to consider the issue rather than quickly reacting. Model for your kids that sometimes taking time to consider options is the best course. Let issues marinate in your mind. Encourage your children to take time to think about issues too.

Do you want your child using fury with their friends and teachers or when they have a problem? Maintaining our calm is good for our health and good for our kids. We are our children's models for how to handle everything from an annoyance to a crisis.

Scaffolding Success

At the garden center, the plants are marked with the ideal conditions for their growth. Some need shade, others sun. They all need food, light and to be left alone for long stretches of time.

What would have been the ideal conditions needed for you to grow and thrive when you were a kid?

Our children do not come with labels listing their foolproof environments for fostering growth. As we get to know our children and remember what it was like to be their age, we can develop an understanding of their needs.

One universal need is to feel successful. People gain this feeling through experience and not only with encouraging words. If a child gets half the answers correct on a math test and feels like a failure, a parent's insistence that she is a great mathematician will not make the child feel successful. The child feels frustrated. The parent should not praise with empty compliments. The child will just think that the parent is just clueless.

Lacking imagination, a parent may not use empty praise but instead find fault in the child's lousy math score, emphasizing the deficits.

But how about if a parent focuses on the answers that were right on the test rather than wrong to examine what went well and help the children focus on how they can apply that success more broadly? When my children were dissatisfied with their grades, I would ask, "What did you learn?" Answers included, I need to study harder. I should have asked for extra help from my teachers. I should not have stayed up so late.

Humans cannot make adjustments and change until we have first identified what the problem is. Rather than condemning, parents can facilitate discussions to evaluate ideas, encourage progress and create solutions.

In the classroom, teachers are aware that children cannot jump from the first floor to the hundredth floor. The progress we engineer is called scaffolding. Once the edifice is completed, the scaffolds can be removed. Teachers support students in learning something new based on what they already can do or know.

When trying to help children feel successful, parents often praise the wrong stuff, saying, "You're so smart." If children are told they possess an inborn talent or genius, they are less likely to take risks and work diligently. They don't want to risk their perceived omniscience, their titular "genius" status by revealing they are pretty inept when trying something new. So they may stick to the safe and the known.

Praising the wrong way may send the message that our children are so smart that they don't have to break a sweat and work hard. Another potential detrimental outcome to praising innate gifts is giving our children the wrong impression that they are somehow superior to others. No one likes an elitist kid with false notions about their supposed special skills.

Progress takes time and the process is step by step. Goals should be attainable and successes should be praised with an emphasis on effort over talent. When children are acknowledged for their diligence, they are more likely to persevere.

When children reach a point of success, they often reach outward to see if parents and teachers are satisfied. Instead, they should be encouraged to develop a habit of first checking in with themselves to cultivate that internal sense of satisfaction. Ideally, children gain their feeling of success within themselves and not exclusively from the feedback of the adults and other people around them. After all, we are available to ourselves at every moment of life to potentially provide support and reassurance. Parents should actively help their children establish and fortify an encouraging voice in their own minds.

Children can be asked how they feel about their performance before the parent chimes in with a compliment. We all benefit from developing honest appraisals of ourselves before seeking others' opinions. When your child is with you, encourage a discussion of goals and nurture a sense of pride with internal self-praise. At the same time, include a gentle reminder that bragging to friends or siblings is forever unappealing. But in front of us, let our children boast away.

To Praise or not To Praise?

You're great at that! Super job! You're better than me at doing that!

Where did all of the gushing praise come from? I don't remember hearing any of it as a kid. At all. Back in my day, teachers and parents kept the compliments to a minimum. We had to strive hard to snag a compliment. And when we heard one, it counted.

Maybe all of the adults of today are trying to fill the air with compliments to make up for that praise famine we had when we were growing up. But we want to make our kids feel good while maintaining our credibility. If we praise everything the kids do, then they think we have no gauge for true quality.

One basketball coach told the team, "You are all champions!" He was a fountain of compliments. The coach wanted to communicate that the kids were great just the way they were. The kids never knew what they needed to improve. But the kids knew they needed to progress and the compliments lost meaning. The team considered the coach to be a know-nothing.

The next year's coach used praise sparingly. When a kid was given a nice word, the whole team's eyes opened wide. Wow! The coach said something nice! The words meant something because the kids believed it when they heard it.

Praise with words that you might use to compliment another adult. Avoid flowery language and superlatives. Praise the effort when your child exerts it. Try not to compliment by comparing your child to others, especially siblings. Your kid is already well versed in how she compares with others. A comment from you just compounds the pain. Occasionally ask your child, "How do you think you did?" before offering your own assessment.

If your child consistently provides a negative view of their performance, try to distinguish if this is out of humility or a developing negative self-perception. If your child is too humble to self-praise, that is to be lauded. If you suspect that your child is down on herself, find an activity where your child feels successful.

If your child has joined the soccer league but has very little talent for the sport, shop around for something that your child does well. The happiest kids I have met were experts at something.

How can a great activity be found? Some parents take their kids with them when they perform volunteer work. Other parents take their kids to the orchestra and say, "Choose an instrument and you can take music lessons." I once spent time with three brothers who took care of the snakes in their parents' pet store. They knew so many details about the snakes that they were radiant with pride as they described them to me. Their accomplishments were real and the compliments they received were credible, though not needed for that good feeling of success.

When a child overhears you complimenting them to another person, the nice words seem more true than if they are delivered directly to the child. If a child is in another room listening, tell the person you are talking to about something wonderful your child did.

Like most things, moderation is good and extremes are to be avoided. What kind of compliments would you like to hear if you were a kid? "You're as smart as Einstein!" may make you feel worse than you did before hearing it. You know it's an exaggeration and leading to unrealistic expectations. The occasional "Nice job kid!" is much more easy on the ears.

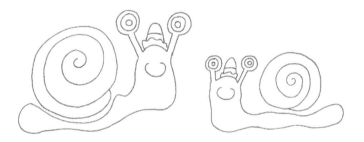

Are We the Barber or the Chef?

Parenting is trial and error. Two parents mix their DNA together and – voila! – out pops a child with traits that may have been passed down from ancestors you never even met. A parent's job, like a good manager or coach, is to bring out the best in their team, their children.

The spectrum of parenting styles runs from the barber on one side to the chef on the other. A barber snips away to eliminate what is not wanted. A chef mixes and adjusts ingredients to maximize deliciousness.

Barber parenting aims to remove or suppress the traits that do not appeal to the parent. A child talks too much at the dinner table? The barber tells her to stay silent.

The chef adjusts and alters by adding flavors. The dish needs a kick? Add some lemon and garlic. The child delivers one monologue after another at the dinner table? The chef explains the art of conversation as a tennis game. One player hits the conversational ball over the net. Then after some talking, tosses the ball back so that the conversation flows. Instead of saying, "Be quiet!" to the child and cutting off the speaking, provide advice and promote understanding so that your child can enjoy the interplay of conversation.

At different times, both the chef and barber are called upon. The barber may be urgently needed if a child harms another person. In the words of the bioethical pledge, "Do no harm," is not a suggestion but a rigid rule for all of us.

But don't let the barber show up too often. The barber is more likely to command with harsh chastisements leading our children to experience a sad, desperate feeling that they are less than what we expect.

So most of the time, choose to be the chef, the more active, thoughtful and reflective parent. Children are little people with grand ambitions.

They are our grown-ups-in-training who need our reflective, thoughtful guidance.

Our Kids, Just Like Library Books

When we have children, it's like we have borrowed a book from the library. We bring the book home. As we live with our child for eighteen years, we have the opportunity to read but not write the chapters. Our job is to make sure that all of the pages are present and readable by the time our child becomes an adult.

Parents may not approve of some of the words, phrases, paragraphs or chapters. One chapter may be about your child's passion to become a painter. The parent may think that becoming an accountant is a more appealing career path, and so the artistic talent is discouraged and the artistic words on those life ambition pages are scribbled out. Instead, scrawled in the margins, is the parental demand that the child becomes an accountant.

Another chapter may be written about a child's shyness. The parent crosses that out and enrolls the reluctant child in embarrassing public speaking and acting classes because being an introvert is not acceptable to the parent. The child feels she is a disappointment based on personality characteristics she cannot change.

If a child has musical talent, the lessons and practices that a parent provides will permit the musical pages to remain. If a parent forces a child to play an instrument even though the child lacks the desires to play, the parent attempts to staple in a musical chapter into the child's life. But the child will stop playing once the parents stop nagging. One woman I knew went to Juilliard and Princeton where she played piano competitively. Once she graduated and gained economic independence, she never touched another piano. Despite her parents' determination that she would be a pianist, she had the ultimate decision-making power about the course of her life. She greatly resented her parents for not listening to her desires and wasting her precious childhood time. Just because a child has talent does not mean she should be pushed to excel.

After eighteen years, our child is ready to leave the family nest and become independent. In other words, the book is returned to the library. The world can view the book and see how the parent treated it. Are the pages ripped, scribbled on and wrinkled? Or is every page fully intact?

Remember that we do not write the pages. We just create the climate for the pages' full expression.

Hopefully, you had the opportunity to be who you are without your parents imposing their will upon you or belittling who you are. Our children come into this world with personalities, predilections and thoughts that are their own just like yours are your own. Provide your children with the dignity to blossom and flourish based on their own, rather than your, path.

Stuck but Still Having Fun

So much of life is about the story we tell ourselves. Two people growing up in the same house can have very different life stories. One may recall the hard times, the times she was a victim of wrongdoing and the heartbreak. A sibling in the same home may remember the good times, the traditions and the laughter. The first person emphasizes the negative and the second person feels strengthened by the positive memories.

As parents, we have a great role in emphasizing which narrative our children will emotionally hook into. We are the president of our homes and, just as our president can set a positive or negative tone that will affect the mood and direction of the country, we set the tone in our homes.

One time my kids and I were in the elevator in my parents' building. As the elevator lurched and then stopped, my kids looked at me with alarm and asked what happened. I said, "This is the most exciting day of our lives. Let me call Mom-Mom and Saba (my parents) and tell them what fun we are having." After the call, my parents called the fire department. When I got off the phone, I told my kids that we were going to meet super cool firefighters. While we waited, we sang funny songs. When the firefighters pried open the doors, and we saw that we were between floors and needed to come down by ladder, I cheered and said, "This is truly the best day ever."

Two weeks later, I ran into a woman in my parents' building. She told me that she got stuck on the elevator with her daughters and all three of them cried until the firefighters arrived. She said, "We're still traumatized. That was one of the scariest days of my life."

Even in challenging times, we have the power of a narrator in a novel. We set the tone and have the ability to create a positive climate for growth and fun.

Dodging Landmines

Freedom of choice can seem like a marvelous thing. But for many of us humans, too many choices can lead to overwhelming anxiety.

My mother once said, "Those twenty flavors of ice cream in the ice cream shop, they make kids unhappy. Look at the kids as they are trying to choose. They feel that maybe they should have gotten something else rather than enjoying what they have. It's much easier if you tell your kids something like, 'There's chocolate, vanilla and strawberry. Choose one, and say thank you.'" When people are offered a small selection, they can easily choose a favorite. When the number of options grow, we have a harder time deciding and often feel less satisfied with our choices. Discontentment ensues.

Limiting the range of choices is a good strategy for managing situations that can go in either a calm or explosive direction.

If we take a child into a toy store and then the child breaks down crying because she wants something that she cannot have, this should not be a surprise. Instead of going to the toy store, maybe the child should be offered a few toys to choose from and then choose one. Then the parent goes into the toy store and purchases the toy without the child.

When confronted with choices, children may want it all. This is logical and natural. Their selection process will be eased when we guide them with calm empathy and foresight. Try to suppress reactive judgements when children are struggling. By making the decision-making process easier by limiting choices, the outcome will be predictable and more satisfying.

You, Darling, are a Science Experiment

Children of all ages use the scientific method for figuring out how the world works. A young child may think, "What happens when I drop my spoon off the high chair? It falls to the ground. Daddy then walks over to it and puts it back on my high chair." Lesson learned about gravity, and my dad's role as my servant on this planet.

The budding scientist may then seek to extend the experiment. "Every time I drop the spoon on the ground, my dad seems to get madder and madder. The fourth time I dropped the spoon, my dad turned red and used a loud voice. I provoked a reaction that I maybe found funny or terrifying. If I find it funny, I will keep tossing my spoon. If his rage was terrifying, I will learn that getting furious is the way to react to frustration."

This process has been frequently called testing limits, just like a scientist in the lab who may be trying to figure out the ideal dosage of a new medicine. The child is seeking knowledge to advance her understanding and enhance her navigation of the world. In other words, the process of throwing the spoon is not a provocation to infuriate, but a time for conducting research in the kiddie lab.

Because we are the lab rats in our child's scientific exploration, we need to actively participate in the study while remaining relaxed and cooperative as the data is being gathered. In the case of the dropping spoon, what lesson would we like our child to learn?

After a child does something that a parent does not like, a calm warning should be issued. "Throwing your spoon on the ground is not ok. The spoon is for eating your food. If you do it again, your food and the spoon will be taken away." The second time the spoon is thrown, the child will check to see if you will follow through on your warning. The child will record the notes in the scientific diary of her mind. "Intentionally and repeatedly dropping my spoon is not going to provide satisfying results. My parent calmly removed my food because repeatedly picking up the spoon is not my parent's role. I'm hungry now and should not repeat this experiment."

Remember to keep your consequences deliberate and always follow through.

In the case of a child coming home late, the lesson in your child's mind may be, "I cannot continue to upset my parent by coming home late. My dad remained calm and told me that, as a consequence, I had to clean the entire bathroom. This does not benefit me, so I will think twice before doing it again."

Stay calm, institute a warning and follow through. Expect tears from the tired, frustrated, up-and-coming scientists. As parents, we are helping our kids to understand the world one spoon at a time.

Your Smartphone or Your Kid?

Worse for family relationships than the television or the Wild West of the internet is a parent with a smartphone. Seeing parents stare at their smartphones when they are with their children in diners, at the playground and walking down the street, makes it clear that these devices are clearly interfering with the development of family relationships.

People make choices based on what they want. When parents are choosing to stare at their smartphones rather than engaging in conversations, watching the school play or cheering as their kids go down the slide, it is a loss for the development of the crucial parent-child connection that helps children mitigate stress and feel emotionally secure.

People's preference for smartphone surfing rather than talking to their fellow adults is obvious when you watch adults in a restaurant staring at their phones rather than talking. When adults do it, they are all in agreement that their electronic device is way more stimulating than the present company.

But when kids are facing their parents and their parents are facing the smartphone, unique opportunities are lost. In my observations, the children look docile and defeated, accepting of the fact that their parents find the device more engaging than they could ever be.

When you are with your kids, put your smartphone away and invest your time in your relationship. Send your kids the message that they are more interesting and worthwhile than any electronics.

Down the line when your kids are teenagers who are socially connecting with their friends by texting, make certain times of the day like mealtimes smartphone free. Hopefully you have modeled the need to switch off the phone during family time.

Before you know it, your kids will be grown and you will have uninterrupted time with your beloved smartphone. But while your kids are with you, let them know that you are present and available for active engagement and playful fun.

Gratitude, Not Brat-itude

During my three decades in the classroom, I have taught a broad range of children from the underprivileged to the one percenters. Nearly all of the children needed a substantial dosage of gratitude. Too many seemed to have adopted the attitude, "What have you done for me lately?"

In an age where we are served nearly as much as royalty, it is easy to see the world as a place that owes us. In exchange for that green paper money, people feel entitled to the best. We shop for products and can get exactly what we want. We are served in restaurants and can find the exact dish that will pique the interest of our palate. If what we purchased or ordered does not please us, we will return it. Children are apt to imitate the adults they see whining a variation of, "My needs are not being met!"

A demanding personality is essentially communicating that, "I, the complainer, deserve better. Improvements must be made immediately if not sooner. Snap to it, servant."

As humans, we survive because of our demanding nature. As babies, we demand food and rest while we charm our way into being loved. Our demanding nature is at odds with the development of gratitude. Gratitude may not come naturally. Instead, it often needs to be deliberately constructed within us.

Build gratitude by pointing out the basics. Regularly expound upon the beauty of having shelter. Show your children or read about those who do not have the privilege of a home that protects from the elements. In the grocery store, express your feelings of good fortune that we live in a world where star fruit and edamame can be purchased year-round. We no longer need to hunt. We do not suffer from shortages. We are not in a war zone.

Build gratitude every day. Whenever I passed a screaming parent on the sidewalk, I said to my kids, "Aren't you lucky that is not your mom?" Emphasize the depth of love that is in your home. Children flourish from the love of their families, no matter if a parent, uncle, grandparent or guardian raises them.

A thankful kid is more likely to have good manners, be liked by peers and adults and find that life is a treasure of simple pleasures.

Each Insult Makes a Wound

In Hungary where I lived for six years in the 1990's, kids were labeled. At that time, students received either a black or red dot at the end of every school day. Black was assigned if the teacher wanted to express displeasure and red if all went well. Maybe the red was the favored color because of the decades of communist occupation.

Imagine being eight years old and receiving the dot every afternoon at the close of a school day. An external source, your teacher, tells you if you are good or bad. As you walk home from school, you are either strutting with your red dot or trying to frame a plausible explanation for why you have a black dot.

Conventional teachers and parents teach children to seek their sense of worth in the eyes of others. Am I good at writing? My teacher decides. Am I helpful around the house? My parents will tell me. With this set-up, we may spend the rest of our lives seeking affirmation from outsiders.

Because children's own opinions of their accomplishments and failures are rarely solicited, they may grow up with a skewed vision of themselves. When I hear adults put themselves down, I sometimes ask, "Why do you think that?" Often, the answer is that a teacher or another adult denigrated their ability when they were children. With an insult, adults have the power to negatively change the course of someone's life. "This material is too challenging for you" may cause a child to avoid math, a paintbrush or public speaking. The echo of the insult can reverberate for years.

Children should be encouraged to take an active role in creating their own identities as they resist labeling by others.

When we do need to go negative with our children, the Golden Rule applies. If you had the same issue as your child, how would you like someone to speak to you? Select your words carefully.

Is your child underperforming because of a lack of effort or a lack of talent? If the issue is a lack of effort, provide an example from your life when your effort level increased, and you experienced success. As a kid, I remember being thrilled by Edison's quote that, "Genius is one percent inspiration, ninety-nine percent perspiration." Hard work should involve sweat, Edison affirmed that diligence would pay off.

Some people do not want to consider that their child's lack of success can be attributed to a lack of talent. I once heard a lecturer say that all children have talent but that some lack effort. I responded by saying that if my gym teacher had told me that the only reason I could not make the WNBA was because I did not display enough effort, I would have felt ridiculous and lazy, even though dedicating every moment of my life to basketball training would not have resulted in me as a draft pick.

If your child lacks talent in a certain area, then you can relate to the frustration of the difficulty of solving an algebra equation/ making a lay-up/ drawing a portrait. Discuss the challenge and then come up with a strategy together for maximizing success.

The current expectation that children need to be little Renaissance people who are good at everything is not healthy or realistic. Maintaining our love for ourselves when we fall short of expectations will build resilience and a smoother ride, even when we inevitably slam into those bumps.

Help Kids Like Themselves

When I was a kid, ridiculing a sibling was viewed as normal. Kids were supposed to be kind and cooperative with people outside of the family, such as friends and strangers. Those within the family could be mistreated.

This acceptance of family discord lacks logic. Be mean to those who will stick by you? Be your best self to everyone else? The family, those closest to us who will love us throughout our lives, should have been the people treated the best. Those who are more distant should be the people we were least concerned with. But for some mysterious reason, our cultural norm is that people have the license to treat members of our own families more harshly than those outside our homes.

I lived in Budapest for six years. As I learned Hungarian, I noticed that siblings in Hungarian families speak sweetly, hug and adore each other. When I told them that the normal American siblings fight, the Hungarians reacted with confusion. Why would you ever be mean to your brother or sister? They are the best people! Friends come and go. Families will stick with you for your whole life!

Then I noticed how Americans encourage sibling rivalry by openly comparing their children. People may ask siblings, "Do you guys fight?" Television programs and books are filled with bratty younger siblings and bully older siblings. A common cultural feeling is that people have a need to unload their negativity on their family in order to be positive to the outside world. They say harmful things or mistreat each other in the belief that the negativity must be released. As a kid, I was taught that we have to release our negative emotions at home. Since our families are not going anywhere, they can become the targets.

When family members are tearing each other down, they can cause our self-esteem to become fragile. The home is ideally the place where people feel most secure, most honest and most supported. The inner circle, the family circle, should receive our best, not our worst.

Oreos!

Oreos are my favorite cookies. This may be genetic. My dad hid boxes between his folded shirts in his closet. The cocoa flavor of those crispy chocolaty cookies. The counterpoint of the smooth, sweet cream. Transcendently delicious. Even though I no longer eat Oreos because I understand that processed foods cause cancer, heart disease and diabetes, I still long for them.

But healthy or unhealthy, I tell my "Oreo cookie" tip to everyone who asks me about how to present a difficult issue to a friend, parent, child, student or teacher.

The Oreo cookie has three layers. First start off with saying something positive. Second, speak about the challenging issue. Third, say something related that is positive. The three statements should flow together.

When we start out positive, people feel more open to our ideas because we are describing the good in them. Their ears are more likely to listen and be more receptive to us.

"You are working really hard at keeping your room clean, and it looks great!"

In the second phase, presenting the issue, be direct but not damning.

"I saw a sandwich that was left overnight on your bed. Bugs and mice might come and eat it. Let's keep the food in the kitchen."

Try not to use the accusatory, "You did this/that." When possible, bring in the first person plural, the "we," like in the statement above, "Let's keep the food in the kitchen." If the speaker had said, "You need to keep the food in the kitchen," the child may become defensive or resistant because of the accusing tone.

The third phase is another compliment. Ending with a compliment helps to reassure our children that the parent continues to be on their side.

"I see your room had an upgrade. Those new posters on your wall are really nice. Good choices!"

The Oreo cookie approach, the positive, negative, positive, works exceedingly well. Think of the two positive statements as two cushions sandwiching the critical statement that, all by itself, might be hard to digest.

This method works and provides nearly the satisfaction of three medjool dates (my Oreo-alternative that is my current go-to healthy and delicious dessert) and a cool glass of soy milk. (Yes, I ditched dairy because, along with sugar, it too causes heart disease, cancer and diabetes.)

Slow Down and Savor

We all seem to be rushing. Some invisible force is giving us the message that we need to be in a hurry.

In a rushing mindset, it's no wonder that we continually say, "I don't know where the day/ week/ month went. Time is flying!" Life is short. A lifetime can feel as if it is lasting as long as a daydream if we don't slow down and savor the present moment.

When I have traveled, I notice that in other countries, people seem to have more time. Even though we share the same 24-hour day with the rest of the world, they move through the time in a slower, more relaxed pace. Upon return from my trips, I have instituted different strategies to slow things down.

One way to slow things down is to be a little bored. Sometimes when the day is going too quickly, I might walk the scenic route by taking an extra block, find something visually interesting to stare at for a minute or two, gaze at a beautiful cloud formation or take note of how efficient and amazing our feet are as they carry us from place to place. I pause to absorb the wonders and beauties in our world.

Kids tend to find their chill time with their electronics. Expand their opportunities for chilling by modeling other sources of relaxation, even if it is for only a minute. With the rushing we do, it's easy for life to go by in a blurred frenzy. Pause during a conversation, point out the smell of the maple syrup, the view out the window, the soft velvety fur on the dog's chin. At the beginning, kids may roll their eyes or rush past you. But over time, they will absorb the importance of taking a moment to slow down and savor.

I was teaching about slowing down to my seventh grade students. One of them put it well when she wrote, "I think it's important to slow down because if you continue to rush, you forget that you are having pleasure. You keep thinking about what you are going to do next. You feel that the next thing that you will do is more significant than the present. You can slow down by being mindful. Benefits of being mindful are that you can actually enjoy yourself instead of regretting your past and worrying about your future."

The Golden Mean

Avoid extremes. On one side is excess. On the other side is deficiency. For most things in life, the middle way is the best way.

The Ancient Greeks called it the Golden Mean. Those who follow Confucius and Buddha have a similar idea of following the middle path.

Try to avoid saying "always" and "never." They are rarely useful and can spark emotional volcanoes.

"I will <u>never</u> bring you for a treat again," I have overheard this from parents. A child may react with anguish if she thinks the statement is true. Or the child may ignore the statement because she knows her parent does not follow through on her threats.

"You are <u>always</u> forgetting to empty the trash." If this is true, a reminder system needs to be put in place that does not involve the parent. A weekly note could be put on the child's calendar or family chalkboard to remind her about her chores.

Extreme views are not helpful or wise for dealing with the messiness of life. We need to improvise and use whatever works in different situations. If a child has a bedtime of nine but her uncle is visiting, going to bed at ten for one night is fine. Have the rules in place and be prepared to break them when needed.

By modeling flexibility, your child will adopt more adaptable approaches to issues. This will pay off, especially if your child may be at risk of developing into a judgmental teen. Those who float between extremes and use whatever method works in a particular situation will adapt better to change.

Improvise

In a jazz band, musicians are prepared to switch things up at any moment. As a parent, it's all about improvisation. Those parents that conduct their families like jazz musicians listen to the melody their kids are playing, and then respond with their own enriching tune.

Taking the lead, parents also need to respond to a dramatic change in tune. Family crises might include emergency room stitches after the jump in the pool, the refusal to put on shoes when it's snowing outside, the jealous shriek when not selected to be the lead in the play. Parents are on call to respond as their children's nurses, psychologists, judges and motivational speakers.

Just when we get used to one childhood stage, our children switch things up on us. Right before we have teenagers, our children may seem eager to strike out on their own and be independent, Tom Sawyer style. But then during the teen years, many children regress at home and their behavior at times

resembles the time of the "terrible twos."
The teens need more sleep or they get
grouchy, just like when they were toddlers.

After a minor event, a teen may react with
the panic that, in their world, the sky is
falling. You may feel that this is not an
authentic catastrophe, and you want to tell
your child that everything is ok and it's no
big deal. If you do present a realistic
assessment to your teen, she may act like you
don't get it. She may think, my problem is
reaching catastrophic levels, and my parent
is clueless to think otherwise. There's no use
in consulting with my parent.

Because open communication keeps us close,
we do not want to shut down our
conversations.

Be an instructor rather than a reactor. In the
case of the falling sky, a parent can say, "I am
so sorry that you are going through this. It is
simply awful. Let me know how I can help."
By sympathizing with the anxiety-ridden
teen and not trivializing the problem, a
parent is more likely to be seen as someone
who provides understanding. The lines of

communication remain open because the parent is viewed as being on the same wavelength as the teen. Once understood, the teen will most likely cool down and more calmly communicate.

Remember that anxiety is a desire to control the future. As your child speaks, help her sort out what can be reasonably influenced and what is not controllable.

Sometimes, the anxiety can cause the kind of irritability that feels like your kid is just itching for a fight. When engaged in an argument, sometimes the best course of action is, if possible, to cut the battle by agreeing with your child. As long as by agreeing you are not then consenting to something dangerous, a simple, "I think you're right," can dissolve the ire and lower the emotional temperature in the house. Then change the subject and return to the discussion when everyone's blood pressure has stabilized.

Often teenagers are irrational. A teen may say, "You never take me anywhere," a few days after returning from a vacation.

You may be tempted to point out that your child is an unappreciative brat who does not deserve a vacation. Or you could say something like, "Maybe you think I am not doing enough for you. I get it, and I will try harder." Teens sometimes feel emotionally isolated. They are better at blaming than identifying their needs. By listening carefully, you can hear hints of their desperate need to feel cared for even though they may say, "I can't stand you" as much as, "I love you."

Listen with understanding but never accept abuse.

Parents' feelings are just as important as children's feelings. Parents are not punching bags for their children to get their anger out. If parents become the place where their children pour out their rage, the stage is set for their children to mistreat their next set of loved ones, their future spouse and children. The home should not be the place where people behave badly and mistreat each other.

Teens are growing at a fast rate and trying to

navigate that complicated final passage from childhood to adulthood. This time can feel like the last few miles of the marathon. Teens need our nurturing and our time as much as they did when they were little. If we want our children to speak about what they are going through, we too need to share what is going on in our lives. Otherwise, the persistent questioning of a concerned parent can feel like an exhausting session with a high-octane District Attorney. Converse with your child. Tell them about your day and stories from your past.

Like in jazz, time is needed to refine the tune, shift the tempo, play around and make mistakes that may evolve into a whole new creation. Patiently create the music and keep it playful. Being a teen is filled with mystery, promise and creativity. Parents can ease the way by reassuring their kids that they are playing in the same band, whistling the same tunes and providing accompaniment harmonies on the treacherous and exhilarating expansion toward adulthood.

Allow Do-Overs

Back during elementary school kickball games, when we would kick the air and the ball would whiz past us, we would scream "do-over!" In my family growing up, we offered each other do overs, the chance to "take it back," if something rude was said.

Sometimes we say the wrong thing. Hurtful words can pour from our mouths. When we have the opportunity to "take it back," we can acknowledge that we were so wrong that we would like to reverse time and erase what we said.

Our kids, the grown-ups-in-training, should not be afraid of making mistakes and taking risks. But unfortunately, many children are, because our culture does not forgive errors or failures. This is reinforced by the tidal wave of standardized tests in most schools. The rigid thinking required by the tests communicates to kids that their individual opinion or creative angle is not valued. There is a right answer, and you better figure it out fast, because the timer is on. Chop-chop!

When I spent months preparing my eighth grade students for the standardized tests, rather than teaching them history and English, they were taught to guess the thoughts of the test's' authors rather than develop their own thinking.

Once the tests were over, I wanted my students to break free from feeling punished for being wrong. I modeled that making mistakes was a natural, healthy and essential element along our winding path toward wisdom. When students caught me making mistakes, I gave them extra credit. They loved it when they identified my errors. "I messed up again?" I said, laughed and recorded the extra credit star in my grade book. This ritual had an added benefit of keeping my students in an intensely aware state in the classroom, like we were in the midst of a game show.

I also took time to tell stories that described the many risks, failures and successes in my life. I did not act flawless like many adults did when I was a kid.

So tell loads of stories.

Kids remember anecdotes much more than lectures.

The classic story structure is:

1.   Things used to be like x.
2.   Then y happened.
3.   Now they are like this.

Give them a good story, and your kids will absorb and retain the lesson. They may ask you to tell the story again and again.

Kids, especially teens, know that everyone is flawed. If someone pretends to be perfect, the child cannot relate to their perfect person false front. Admit your screw-ups to your kids. Tell them how you dealt with your issues. We connect through our common, mistake-ridden humanity. What better opportunity is there than a "do over?"

Resourceful Kid

On curriculum night, the helicopter parents are out in full force. They are ready to go into battle for their kids, slay dragons and make certain that their kids do not have to deal with any adversity. This determination to shelter their children from any storm has lead to the news stories that eight percent of parents accompany their children to their first job interviews.

Parents can greatly assist in helping their children gradually become independent. When children are young, parents can stand at the door of a store, give their child money and have their child buy what is needed. Kids can have chores around the house and earn allowance money. The money can be budgeted to meet their needs and save up for something that is desired. In some homes, a percentage of the allowance is given to charity. Kids can research the charity and figure out how to allocate the funds.

When children get older, they can invest some of the money and take on more responsibilities within the home like cooking and cleaning. All of the activities are geared toward having an eighteen year old who can cook meals, clean her home, save, invest, be independent and thrive.

The preparation for independence should not be a mad dash that occurs a few months before she turns eighteen. The preparation for the magical first day of adulthood can begin when she buys her first fruit salad from the corner store at age four.

Make it Playful

Games make life more fun. When ordinary activities morph into games, time goes fast, enthusiasm builds and playful laughter fills the air. Why don't we do it more often?

When it was clean up time in my kindergarten class, we sang a song as we put the toys away. At home, we had a chart, I set the timer and we raced to break our previous record for cleaning up.

Passing pedestrians on the sidewalk, we discussed who deserves the best-dressed award. We created wild and crazy back stories for strangers. When the bus came, we pretended our limo driver had arrived. On the bus, we chose who had the coolest hairdo or looked like our next president.

Games we played include twenty questions, name that tune, guess my number, name the coolest thing you see and I spy. We create our own fun world during mundane activities by playing games we have made up or learned.

Invent Rituals!

Rituals come in many forms but my favorites are new ones. One family I know orders Chinese food when it starts raining and Japanese food when it begins to snow. These traditions are highly anticipated by the kids and relished by the adults.

During traditional holidays like Thanksgiving, creating new rituals will brighten things up. Acting out the Thanksgiving story is a fun activity to do between courses. A few props and a quick script can transform the table into a lively improv group.

Before the big dinner in my family, we write what we are thankful for on slips of paper and bake the slips into bread rolls. We choose one, tear open the roll, read the statement and try to guess who wrote it.

As part of our nighttime ritual, we all say our favorite parts of the day. This may open up a conversation about the day's twists and turns. It also sets up a thought pattern during the day to look out for and prepare to select the day's highlight so that everyone is ready to reveal it at nighttime. By searching for positive events, your child's mind emphasizes the upside rather than becoming mired in negative thinking.

Breakfast in bed on birthdays, creating family music videos of favorite songs, filling a gratitude jar with written notes about great events and having days dedicated to doing what one member of the family wants to do are some of the rituals that can be incorporated into your family.

Those who play together, stay together.

A Tattler's Tales

Early in my teaching career, I saw that giving children individual attention was like giving them M & M's. Each time I said a child's name, I was giving them an invisible, delicious M & M. Once the student ate it, she would want another one. The child would do something else to get the attention focused on her once again.

For children who seek attention, they prefer good attention. However, bad attention is better than no attention.

Children who tell on each other are very hungry for these attention-seeking M & M's. When a child would come over to me and say something like, "Joey is cursing," I responded, "I am so glad that you do not curse." The child would smile and skip away feeling good. The tattler was fishing for a compliment, and she got one. She did not want Joey to be in trouble as much as she sought the reassurance that she was on the right path.

The M & M's are a gift from an external

source. Ideally, children are on the path to receiving M & M's from themselves. The adults in their lives should support children's own internal motivation that builds self-reliance and promotes endless encouragement. If children can learn to rely on themselves for positive messages, they will be able to sail through the world with a happier frame of mind.

The Golden Four

Have you heard yourself or other parents say something like, "My child will be a doctor/ accountant/ astronaut when she grows up?" Some parents would like to dictate their children's future even though many of the jobs that will exist for our kids cannot even be imagined now.

Certain parents want their children to follow in their footsteps. "It worked for me, so it will work for my son."

Other parents would like their child to fulfill their own dreams. "I could not be a judge, but my kid is going to sit up on that bench someday." These parents can't help but imagine their children curing disease, prosecuting malfeasance or conducting a symphony. For a variety of reasons, some parents feel that they are better at making career and life decisions than their own kids. These are often the same parents who would never let others make such decisions for themselves.

How would we feel if we were forced to

choose a career to please someone else?

We want to guide our kids as they choose careers because, along with the love partner they choose, their work life will be a great determiner of their happiness.

At my college graduation party, I had the good fortune of chatting with a friend's dad about the choices ahead. He provided some solid and simple advice that helped me to figure out which job to choose. He said, "Prioritize the following four:

prestige,
money,
power,
&
time.

Then look for a career that matches your priorities."

What was true then is true now. My priorities have not shifted. My order was time, power, money and prestige. Time meant time away from work. Power meant power over my own choices and not power over others, though it can mean either one. The four goals are open to interpretation.

Thinking about the four goals gives young people an opportunity to thoughtfully consider potential careers. After all, people should ideally have a chance to choose where they will eventually punch the clock.

Manners Matter

Having good manners is one area where everyone will be praised. Adults will respond positively and kids will be grateful. Manners are the kindnesses that keep us civilized.

When my mom was little, her parents insisted that she greet the many aunts, uncles and cousins with curtsies and kisses. She detested the formality and time it took to individually greet each one as they sat around the card table every afternoon. My mom resolved that when she was a parent, she would not force us to greet people.

If not through force, how do we instill manners in our children? Through modeling. Emphasizing good manners is a big favor that you are providing for your child. As with all things parenting, you are the role model. When your child sees you holding the door for strangers or picking up someone's dropped scarf and returning it, she will follow in your footsteps as she sees the positive reaction a well-mannered person receives. Although it may not happen overnight, the manners will develop.

Accept Thyself

I love the phrase, "If mama ain't happy, ain't nobody happy." By maximizing our own happiness, we are more likely to have happy kids. This phrase holds true for any parent, teacher or coach.

We are models for our children's own self-acceptance. If we do not love ourselves as we are, our children are unlikely to embrace and love themselves.

A parent may preach self-acceptance from morning until night but nothing beats actually loving yourself as you are.

If you don't already have one, invite a positive, internal narrator into your head. Evict the gloomy, grouchy, never satisfied voice that remind me of those two guys crabbing it up in the balcony of "The Muppet Show." An easily satisfied, positive voice builds the confidence needed to face challenges and enjoy our brief time on this earth.

Find a way to embrace yourself just as you

are. Set the bar low for giving yourself compliments. I used to have to be flawless to earn a compliment from myself. These days I am much happier. I cheer myself on when I make a good cup of coffee, help out a friend or cook a good meal. It's easy for me to earn my own praise.

Be your own best friend and cheerleading squad. Life is more fun that way.

... & one more thing.

Snuggle lots. Way, way more than you do now.

Our kids get to a certain age and those warm cuddles are not to be had. It's a snuggle famine out there until grandkids may one distant day come for a too-brief visit.

So savor the time you can cuddle and feel that love.

Dedication

This book is dedicated to my dad who, as a parent, was part panda, part curmudgeon and all heart. During the day, Dad was a physician activist dedicated to widening access for indigent health care, prenatal care and cancer treatment. With one of the best brains I ever encountered, Dad's mind had one unfortunate blind spot. With a complete unawareness of nutrition, Dad consumed immense quantities of diet soda, sticks of butter and steaks. He passed away at 73 after decades of diet-related diseases like hypertension, diverticulitis, diabetes and, in the end, pancreatic cancer.

All of Dad's unhealthy food addictions began in childhood. To increase the spread of nutritional awareness before food addictions form, 10% of this book's profits will go to the Coalition for Healthy School Foods, a nonprofit that educates children in high need schools about the dangers of deadly food. Currently, 675,000 Americans die every year from diseases linked to eating bad food. CHSC is part of the solution.

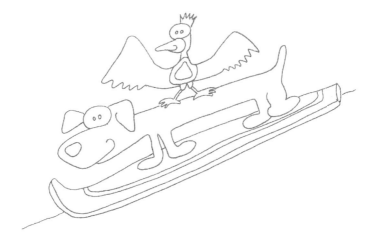

facebook.com/BeTheParentYouWishYouHad